SPAIN

GALLERY BOOKS
An Imprint of W. H. Smith Publishers Inc.
112 Madison Avenue
New York City 10016

This edition first published in U.S.
in 1990 by Gallery Books,
an imprint of W.H. Smith Publishers, Inc.
112 Madison Avenue, New York, New York 10016

ISBN 0-8317-0264-8

Printed and bound in Spain

For rights information about the photographs in
this book please contact:

The Image Bank
111 Fifth Avenue, New York, NY 10003

Producer: Solomon M. Skolnick
Writer: F. Lisa Beebe
Design Concept: Lesley Ehlers
Designer: Ann-Louise Lipman
Editor: Sara Colacurto
Production: Valerie Zars
Photo Researcher: Edward Douglas
Assistant Photo Researcher: Robert V. Hale
Editorial Assistant: Carol Raguso

Title page: All the color and vibrance
of seductive Seville is echoed in the
beautiful tilework of its attractive *Plaza
de España. Opposite:* Madrid's sump-
tuous eighteenth-century Royal Palace
is the creation of Italian designers
Juvara and Sachetti.

When Joseph Bonaparte briefly ruled Spain from Madrid's Royal Palace (the *Palacio de Oriente*) in the early nineteenth century, Napoleon deemed his brother's lodgings better than his own at the Tuileries. *Below:* Considered one of Europe's more opulent palaces, the Royal Palace has some 2,800 rooms filled with art objects, antiques, and hundreds of impressive tapestries; the Throne Hall is one of the rooms open to the public.

S pain: The very word resounds with a certain majesty that is echoed in the Spanish bearing itself. The set of the shoulders, the vaguely regal inclination of the head convey a strong reverence for personal dignity and honor. *Amor propio* (self-respect) governs all behavior. At once staunchly individualistic and dedicated to tradition, a Spaniard may well claim to be a free thinker, but would never, ever drink vermouth after dinner (everyone knows it's strictly an aperitif!).

The loyalties of Spaniards adamantly break down into regional, provincial, municipal, and even village allegiances. Now divided into 17 regions all flexing their autonomous muscles and reviving their distinctive customs, legends, and in some cases even languages, Spain first coalesced into a country in 1492 when the Catholic monarchs Ferdinand and Isabella finally triumphed over the Moors of southern *al-Andalus* and gathered together a medieval patchwork of contentious kingdoms and elastic caliphates in a

This page, top to bottom: Recently restored, Madrid's mid-nineteenth-century *Teatro Real* (Royal Theater) has reverted to its original role as Opera House after serving for many years as the venue for concerts by the Spanish National Orchestra. Occupying the heart of Madrid's cobblestoned *Plaza Mayor* is the seventeenth-century statue of Philip III by Giovanni da Bologna. A symbol of the enduring Spain, Madrid's *Plaza Mayor,* once the site of bullfights and the Inquisition's autos-da-fé, is now ringed with cafés and souvenir shops, and in summer hosts numerous open-air concerts and theatrical performances; every Sunday morning it hosts a stamp and coin market.

prototype of today's Spain. Five hundred years later, Spanish unity remains highly translucent, and today's Basque considers himself to be far more different from a Catalán than, say, a Bostonian from a native of Kankakee, Illinois. Since full-fledged democracy returned to the country in 1976, Spain's response to the long-standing, fragmented loyalties has been to distribute power among 52 provinces and 17 autonomous regional governments, including the Balearic Islands in the Mediterranean and the Canary Islands off of northern Africa.

Despite the bravado inherent in the Spanish character, until recently the country suffered from a national inferiority complex. "Africa begins at the Pyrenees" was a notion coined by northern Europeans to suggest that the countries of the Iberian Peninsula were a part of Europe in geography only. Following a brutal Civil War, Franco's rule isolated Spain on the sidelines of the twentieth century, and many Spaniards came to believe the northern European notion, viewing the Pyrenees as both a physical and psychological boundary between northern progress and southern stagnation. The French, the Germans, the British, the Americans, and

This page, top to bottom: Running from the *Plaza de España* to the *Plaza de la Cibeles,* the *Gran Vía* is the boundary between the old city to the south and Madrid's newer, northern reaches. Madrid, situated about as far away from the sea as you can get in Spain, is very fond of its diminutive Manzanares River. From "Kilometer Zero" in Madrid's *Puerta del Sol,* national roads radiate to all corners of the country; like New York's Times Square, this is the traditional gathering place for revelers on New Year's Eve.

Above: The idealistic Don Quijote is Spain's leading literary legend. *Right:* Along with his bumbling but pragmatic sidekick Sancho Panza, Don Quijote greets passersby in Madrid's *Plaza de España.*

Plaza de la Cibeles and its grandiose *Palacio de Comunicaciones* (Central Post Office) is a famed Madrid landmark. *Opposite:* Dramatically illuminated at night, the ancient mother-goddess Cybele is the focal point of the Cibeles Fountain.

numerous others, the Spanish felt, could simply do everything better than they could.

After Franco's death, his hand-picked successor, King Juan Carlos, rescued the nation from political uncertainty and orchestrated a return to democracy within a constitutional monarchy. The national self-esteem was now well on its way to recovery. From a provincial, strait-laced nation where divorce was prohibited and public discussion of politics taboo, Spain made, in one fleeting decade, a quantum leap to permissive programming on television and a range of political options for every ideological persuasion.

After joining the European Economic Community in 1986, Spain's economy grew at nearly twice the rate of that of most other European countries. Swift and unswerving, its political and economic progress surprised many, not least of all the Spaniards themselves, and the overall mood is one of exuberant self-confidence as Spain jockeys for position within the Common Market and among the world's prominent nations. Meanwhile, a diversity of climates, scenery, and cultural and historical influences unmatched by most other European countries annually attracts a tourist population exceeding the country's own 40 million inhabitants. The visiting hordes come to marvel at the panoramic riches ranging from the rolling, green

This page, top to bottom: Charles III built Madrid's *Puerta de Alcalá* to beautify the city's eastern entrance. Madrid's palatial Central Post Office graces one of the capital's busiest intersections. Between the Prado and the Spanish Parliament stands the Palace Hotel, one of Madrid's most luxurious and lively.

This page: Columbus is to Spain as George Washington is to America. Seemingly every village, town, and city boasts his passing presence and pays him tribute in some way. In Madrid he is celebrated with a statue, a monument, and the eponymous *Plaza de Colón* (Columbus Square).

This page: Madrid's blend of traditional and contemporary architecture reflects the city's spirit. The Prado enshrines the artistic wealth Spain's long line of monarchs while the Monument to the 1978 Constitution (below) salutes the ultimate triumph of democracy.

Alcalá de Henares is the birthplace of Cervantes. In its sixteenth-century heyday its university rivaled Salamanca's as the most venerable seat of learning. *Below:* Madrid's Discovery of America monument in the *Plaza de Colón* commemorates Spain's bold ventures into the New World.

Notable among the gleaming structures of Madrid's northern reaches are (clockwise from top left) the *Torre de Madrid,* Picasso Tower, and the geometric sculpture of the Azca area.

hills of Galicia and the snow-tipped Picos de Europa in the north to the arid, olive-rich terrain of the south. They come for the sun and sea, the food and wine, the flamenco and bulls, and for the crisp, clear Mediterranean light that illuminates a land believed to have been inhabited as many as 14,000 years ago.

Around 3000 B.C. the Iberians came across the Strait of Gibraltar and the Ligurians across the Pyrenees from Italy. In 1100 B.C. the Phoenicians filtered in through the southern coast, and in 900 B.C., following a primitive touristic impulse, the Celts crossed over from France and Britain spurning the northern

This page: Scattered among the trees, gardens, and paths of Madrid's *El Retiro* park are impressive works of art and architecture.

winters in favor of the warm Spanish sun. Succeeding centuries brought the Greeks, Romans, Visigoths, and Moors, who during the course of their lengthy reign (711 to 1492) elaborated on the Roman flair fo luxury and fine living to fashion the most elegant and technologically sophisticated civilization of its day.

After the defeat of the Moors by the Catholic monarchs Ferdinand and Isabella and the unification of Spain in 1492, the country built a glorious New World empire that shone brightly for just over a century. The British defeat of the Armada in 1588 heralded the beginning of the empire's end, and the continual drain of national talent at the brutal hands of the centuries long Inquisition eventually brought Spain to its knees. Recovery was slow and sporadic, and just when Spain was again beginning to show signs of promise early in this century, the Civil War set it reeling. Happily, as the century draws to a close, Spain's stock is on the rise again

Gracious and hospitable to visiting foreigners, Spain dazzles them with diversity. From the red-headed bagpipe players of the once-Celtic north to the dark Latin beauties of the once-Moorish south, the eclectic

This page: The *Plaza de Toros de las Ventas* is the capital's bullring. With the bullfight again gaining in popularity, the sport's colorful posters are in great demand both among aficionados and souvenir-seeking tourists. Majestic and silent, Madrid's bullring awaits the next spectacle. *Opposite:* Rooted in the mythical underpinnings of the ages, the Spanish bullfight is an emotion-charged event suffused with color, pomp, and pageantry. *Below:* Before the first confrontation between man and bull, all participants in the ritual parade around the ring.

historical currents that built the nation are written all over its faces. Similarly, its cuisines, customs, folk arts, and tradition vary markedly from province to province, region to region. Taken as a whole, Spain is Europe's third-largest country (after the U.S.S.R. and France) and its second most mountainous (after Switzerland). Its capital, Madrid situated at 600 meters (about 2,000 feet), is Europe's highest.

Located smack in the center of the country, Madrid had capitalhood thrust upon it during the reign of Philip II in the mid-sixteenth century. Ever since, it has been trying to steer a common course through Spanish diversity. Unlike such capitals as Bonn and Washington D.C. where the social life takes a back seat to the seriousness of government, Madrid is a sophisticated, cosmopolitan city whose motto should be "Fun for all and all for fun." When it comes to government, banking, and the administrative minutiae of running a country, Madrid does a commendable job; when it comes to diversion, it continually sets new standards of excellence. Catering to almost four million *madrileños* are well over 8,000 bars and cafés—or about one for every 600 residents.

This page, top to bottom: Philip II conceived *El Escorial* to be part monastery and part royal residence. Complete in 1584, its library, second only to the Vatican's, holds the writings of St. Augustine, Alfonso the Wise, and Santa Teresa. Its Pantheon of the Kings holds the remains of all the Spanish kings since Charles V, with the exception of Philip V and Ferdinand VI. *Opposite:* Reputed to be the largest in the world, the cross at the *Valle de los Caídos* near *El Escorial* marks the site of a vast underground basilica containing the tomb of General Franco.

Some 2,000 castles dot the Spanish countryside. Among the 100 or so worth visiting is the well-preserved Guadamur Castle near Toledo, dating back to the fifteenth century. *Below:* Set amidst an impressively craggy landscape, the romantic city of Cuenca is noted for its *casas colgadas* (hanging houses).

This page: Situated on a loop of the Tagus River, Toledo, a former capital of Spain, passed the wisdom of the ancient Greek, Roman, and Arab worlds on to Christendom. Until the onset of the Inquisition, its Christians, Jews, and Moors lived together in peaceful, productive harmony.

Above, left to right: Toledo's Cathedral was superimposed on a Moorish mosque that in turn had been superimposed on a church of the Goths. The twelfth-century Moorish gate, *Puerta del Sol,* was rebuilt by the Hospitallers in the fourteenth century. Only pedestrians can enter Toledo via the *Puente de San Martín,* which spans the Tagus. *Below:* The Gothic cloisters of *San Juan de los Reyes* date from the time of the Catholic monarchs.

Above: Toledo's thirteenth-century mudéjar *Santiago del Arrabal* church features a Moorish tower and recessed brickwork on the outside. *Right:* From 1579 until his death in 1614, El Greco lived in Toledo; the El Greco House and Museum is so named because he lived and died in part of the palace that once stood there.

Before democracy was reinstated, the national slogan was "Spain is different." One way in which Spain differed most notably—and still does—was in the hours that it kept. Simply put, the country divides its day differently. Lunch is typically eaten between 2 P.M. and 4 P.M. (and often takes the full two hours) and dinner between 10 P.M. and midnight. Since Spain joined the Common Market there has been much talk of synchronizing the national clock with that of other European nations. But as Spanish working hours slowly adapt to the international norm, Spanish social life clings to the old, late-night ways. Loathe to call it a night at a reasonable Continental hour, *madrileños* deem it appropriate to begin the festivities sometime past midnight—any night of the week!

Along with government and diversion, art has long been a forte of the Spanish capital. The boulevard stretching from Madrid's Plaza de la Cibeles to its Museo Nacional Centro de Arte Reina Sofía, the city's repository of contemporary art, is arguably the world's richest artistic mile. Here stands the well-endowed Prado, owner of over 6,000 canvases, with collections of Goya and Velázquez that amount to a crash course in the Spanish temper. Across

This page, top to bottom: Segovia's late-Gothic cathedral is fashioned of beautiful, warm-colored stone. Disney based his castle in *Snow White and the Seven Dwarfs* on Segovia's fairy-tale-like *Alcázar,* wherefrom in 1474, Princess Isabella set forth to be crowned Queen of Castile in Segovia's *Plaza Mayor.* The summer palace of the Bourbon monarchs, *La Granja* near Segovia is a modest rendition of Versailles.

Above: Hannibal's westernmost conquest, Salamanca, a city of golden sandstone structures, is situated on the Tormes River. *Below, left to right:* Salamanca's Gothic New Cathedral is adjacent to its Romanesque Old Cathedral. Salamanca boasts the most beautiful *Plaza Mayor* in the land.

Above, left to right: Salamanca's *Iglesia San Martín* combines Romanesque and Renaissance elements. Sitting on a high ridge flanked by ramparts is the imposing castle at Peñafiel. The Plateresque facade of Salamanca's most famed university building contains likenesses of the Catholic monarchs amidst an ornamental abundance of literary, pagan, and religious symbols. *Below:* Within this slate-roofed castle Simancas are the National Archives.

In a country brimming with stunning cathedrals, León's stands out as an exquisite example of Spanish Gothic architecture; also magnificent are its kaleidoscopic stained glass windows. *Below:* Fashioned of narrow pinkish bricks by Moorish bricklayers, the castle of Coca is encircled by a deep moat and adorned with octagonal turrets, merlons, and elaborate castellation.

the way, in the Palacio de Villahermosa, several hundred masterworks from the famed Von Thyssen collection will be installed by the end of 1991. Reverently housed in a Prado annex is Picasso's *Guernica,* which returned to Spain with democracy and is both a re-minder of the devastation Spain suffered during its Civil War and a tribute to its remarkable comeback.

Every major city nowadays seems to have its Times Square equivalent. In Madrid it is the Puerta del Sol, site of Kilometer Zero, where all national roads begin. Nearby is the *Palacio de las Cortes,* the parliament building, whose bronze lions were forged from melted-down cannons that saw service in the African Wars. Here, on February 23, 1981, Antonio Tejero, a member of the Civil Guard, held the Spanish government hostage for some 18 hours. No one was harmed, Tejero capitulated, and the central government resumed its course from Madrid's *Cortes.*

Ever piqued that Madrid sets national policies is Barcelona, Spain's second-largest city. As the capital of Catalonia, this city of almost two million is redefining itself within the new political framework at home and the new economic climate in Europe.

This page, top to bottom: Among the carved figures adorning Burgos's eleventh-century *Arco de Santa María* are those of Emperor Charles V and local hero El Cid. Viewed from the tower of the ruins of *San Pedro de Arlanza* Monastery, the scenic delights of Burgos Province unfold all around. The bastions of *Peñaranda de Duero* formed part of the fortified line built by the Christians along the Duero River. *Opposite:* A repository of artistic treasures, curios, and folklore, Burgos's thirteenth-century cathedral (Spain's third largest) is considered by the city's inhabitants to be El Cid's mausoleum.

Across the centuries, many thousands of pilgrims have made their way to Santiago de Compostela and the Cathedral housing St. James' remains; on July 25, the Feast Day of St. James, the city swells with the faithful come to join in the municipal celebration. *Below:* Part of the festivities is the swinging of the *Botafumeiro,* the giant censer of 1602.

"Cuando Franco"—as the Spanish say whenever they refer to that era so recent in time yet so far away in spirit—the use of the Catalan and Euskera (Basque) languages and the celebration of regional festivals were banned. No wonder then that with the demise of the Franco regime and the establishment of regional autonomies, such manifestations of regional pride rushed to the surface of Spanish life with renewed vigor.

In Barcelona, the signs of the newly autonomous times are increasingly in Catalan, the indigenous and now second official language of Catalonia.

On the isthmus at La Coruña stands the Tower of Hercules, the world's only remaining Roman-era lighthouse—and it still works. *Below:* A key shipping center since Roman times, La Coruña's active commercial port tins, cures, and salts the local fishermen's catches. For travelers, it is a good departure point for touring Galicia's Rias Atlas.

This act of linguistic rebellion underscores the enduring rivalry between Catalonia and Castile, and more specifically, between Barcelona and Madrid.

Amazingly, Barcelona made great strides during the dictatorship and served as a Mediterranean window on the world that was passing the rest of Spain by. Books banned throughout the country made their way to Barcelona bookstores. When avant-garde art was denounced in Madrid, Barcelona staged exhibitions that stunned the national sensibility.

When the dictatorship ended, however, the tables turned and Madrid gained the momentum. The *movida madrileña*, a social and cultural renaissance touching all aspects of Madrid life, thrust the city onto center stage. Fashion designers, filmmakers, writers, and businesspeople launched from Madrid catapulted into the international limelight. Adolfo Domínguez dressed "Miami Vice's" Don Johnson for a season, Pedro Almodóvar conquered Cannes, Camilo José Cela won the Nobel Prize for literature, and Mario Conde earned a worldwide reputation for fending off hostile takeovers and putting together highly profitable deals.

Meanwhile, Barcelona suffered from a serious case of back-seat status. But not for

This page, top to bottom: Asturia's coastline meets the Cantabrian Sea. Among the alpine vistas of Asturia's 8,000-foot-high *Picos de Europa,* Spain reaches its scenic apex. Rooted in Roman times, Pamplona is said to have been founded by Pompey; fiercely independent, the *pamplonicos* signed their own bill of rights known as the *Fueros* in the thirteenth century and still live by them today.

This page: Ever since Hemingway immortalized Pamplona's *Fiesta de San Fermín* in *The Sun Also Rises*, the world has come to associate this city in Navarra with the annual Running of the Bulls that takes place from July 6th through the 20th. The two-minute daily run through the streets of Pamplona passes by the City Hall (above, right) en route to the bullring (below).

Preceding page: Among the neolithic legacies found throughout Spain are numerous dolmens like this one at Biescas in Aragón. *Below:* The Pyrenees are prime skiing territory in winter and a scenic retreat in summer.

Above: As the sun sets on the Ebro River at Zaragoza, the towers and domes of the city's *Basilica de Nuestra Señora del Pilar* carve a distinctive silhouette against the darkening sky. *Below, left to right:* The focal point of Trujillo's *Plaza Mayor* is the monument to Pizarro, *conquistador* of Peru. Many of Spain's *conquistadores* came from the region of Extremadura; here in Medellín they honor native son Hernán Cortés. Jerez de los Caballeros, home of Vasco Núñez de Balboa, discoverer of the Pacific, is distinguished by the beautiful sixteenth-century San Bartolomé church.

ong. Buckling down to business, the city set its sights on the 1992 Summer Olympic Games and looked to its traditional strong suits—innovative art, architecture, and design—to reassert itself as a formidable center for cutting-edge culture. While prevailing practice is to honor artists only after their death, Barcelona is more inclined to seize the artistic moment. The new Antoni Tapies Foundation, which celebrates the prolific contribution of this Catalan abstract expressionist to contemporary culture, has joined the city's Picasso and Miró Museums in offering visitors a coherent account of art in our times.

Ever bold and daring in its architectural vision, Barcelona continually expands upon its splendid Gothic and modernist (the Catalan version of Art Nouveau) foundations. Antonio Gaudí, the modernist master who conceived the city's *Sagrada Familia*—a twentieth-century cathedral of medieval proportions that is inching its way to controversial completion—gave the city an enduring taste for architectural dash and verve. Among those indulging that taste and reshaping the municipal contours for the twenty-first century are Arata Isozaki, Richard Meier, Gae Aulenti, Norman Foster, Victorio Gregotti, I. M. Pei, and native son Ricardo Bofill.

This page, top to bottom: Former capital of Rome's Lusitania province, Mérida boasts many important Roman remains; among them, this theater dating from 24 B.C. Mérida's *Museo Nacional de Arte Romano,* built around the excavations of a Roman wall, contains Roman artifacts unearthed in the area. Sixty granite arches long, Mérida's *Puente Romano,* dating from the days of Trajan, stands up to the rigors of modern traffic across the Guadiana River.

Meanwhile, in the Spanish countryside, the windmills of La Mancha, the castles of Castile, the Romanesque churches along the centuries-old pilgrimage route to Santiago de Compostela, the olive groves of Andalusia, and the shepherds, vineyards, and fields of grain scattered throughout the land paint a timeless portrait of Spain, a nation with one foot firmly planted in yesterday and the other poised on the threshold of tomorrow. In the narrow streets of Toledo, the medieval vistas savored by El Greco mingle with the strains of Madonna's latest. In the rural recesses of Andalusia guitar-toting gypsies serenade vintners on the verge of international joint ventures. Here an

Above: Córdoba's eighth-century *Mezquita,* second only in size to the mosque at Mecca, contains at its core a sixteenth-century cruciform church. *Left:* Don Quijote did battle with just such a windmill in La Mancha.

ve, left to right: The fourteenth-century Tower of the Calahorra in Córdoba houses a museum of the city's history. Inside Córdoba's *zquita,* nearly 1,000 diverse columns support row upon row of double arches in an architectural expression of infinity. Seville's crescent-*ped Plaza de España,* built for the Spanish-American Exhibition in 1929, houses government offices in its Renaissance-style structures. *ow:* Outside Córdoba's Moorish walls is the marble figure of the famous Arab philosopher Averroës.

Preceding page: The alcoves of Seville's *Plaza de España* are adorned with tiled murals dedicated to each of Spain's provinces. *Below:* Five graceful, tiled bridges span the *Plaza de España's* arch-shaped lagoon.

Seville's Cathedral is Christendom's third largest. Its planners ordained that it "never should have its equal." *Below:* Inside Seville's Cathedral is one of the several alleged tombs of Columbus. *Opposite:* Linking the old and new towns of Ronda, where bullfighting on foot began, is the *Puente Nuevo,* spanning a vertiginous 400-foot gorge.

there, yesteryear's withering castles and monasteries are reborn as posh *paradores* (government-run hotels in rural areas) for today's upscale tourists. And when not staging the national *corrida*, many a bullring in the land resounds with rock and heavy metal.

Yes, Spain is changing. And it is not. Its national self-esteem restored, the country is no longer embarrassed by such indigenous traditions as the bullfight and flamenco. Attendance at *corrida* is on the rise as a new crop of bullfighters is revitalizing the national spectacle. Though the bullfight and flamenco have become national symbols, they are really native to the south; and although northern Spaniards attend *corridas* and occasionally indulge in the fiery Andalusian song and dance, theirs are other pastimes, other folk traditions not to be eclipsed by the national stereotype. Flamenco is the legacy of the south's Moors, Jews, and gypsies. The northern Spaniards swear by the *jota*, a jig-like dance rooted in Celtic cavorting. In Catalonia they dance the *sardana*. And everywhere they know the *bolero*.

The bullfight is perhaps the only true, though tenuous, common denominator in this highly diversified country. Still, the Basques prefer the game of *jai alai*, and most Spaniards are more hooked on soccer. With the cult of the bull at least as old as the Minotaur, every Spanish *corrida* is suffused with the epic

This page, top to bottom: Casares and Arcos de la Frontera (center) are two of Andalusia's famed *pueblos blancos* (white villages). Celebrities and luminaries congregate at Puerto Banus on the Costa del Sol.

Castillo de la Estrella in Málaga Province. *Below:* Málaga is the municipal cornerstone of Spain's Costa del Sol.

Jaen's Renaissance Santa María Cathedral dominates the narrow streets and petite squares of the old town. *Below:* Granada, the las stronghold and longest-running kingdom of the Moors, and its crowning jewel, *La Alhambra*, are set against the backdrop of the Sie Nevada. *Opposite:* Pools and fountains were the supreme indulgence of Moorish men of means, and *La Alhambra* is laced with them.

Preceding page: Gardens like the *Alhambra's Jardín de Lindaraja* were another Moorish passion. *Below:* A fish pond flanked by hedges of myrtle reflects the fine stalactite vaulting of *La Alhambra's Patio de los Arrayanes.*

emotions of millenia. Reviled by some as a morbid exercise in death and hailed by others as an affirmative celebration of life, the bullfight is both and, as such, reflects a national temper that tends to extremes.

At the same time, Spaniards exhibit an acute appreciation for the subtleties that make a celebration of everyday life. Before taking cutlery in hand, they often pause to savor the aroma of their meal. It enhances the pleasure, they say. And with at least five distinctive regional cuisines to choose from and some of the best seafood in the world, much pleasure awaits at the Spanish table. Madrid's restaurants, while about as far from the sea as one can get in this country, offer an abundance of fresh marine produce trucked into the capital daily from all watery corners of the country. The cuisine of the Basques, influenced by neighboring France, is often proclaimed Spain's finest. But the competition is fierce. Catalan cuisine, seasoned with French and Italian influences, has many staunch advocates. So do the roast lambs and suckling pigs of Castile, the stews of Asturias, the paella of Valencia, and the sweet prawns and crabs of Galicia. Nationally speaking, the seasonings are subtle; the olive oils fruity and fresh; and the meat, game, and fish done to a succulent turn.

This page, top to bottom: On March 19, the Feast of St. Joseph, Valencia sprouts countless papier-maché figures poking fun at politics, people, and life; at night these figures are set on fire and the city appears to be burning down. Noted for its finely crafted ceramics, Valencia has installed in the eighteenth-century *Palacio del Marqués de Dos Aguas* the National Ceramic Museum containing over 5,000 exhibits tracing the history of the art. El Parterre, Valencia.

Above: Artists, *literati,* and connoisseurs of fine Mediterranean scenery flock to Cadaqués on the Costa Brava. *Right:* A castle, a secluded cove, the Mediterranean—an enticing Costa Brava fantasy.

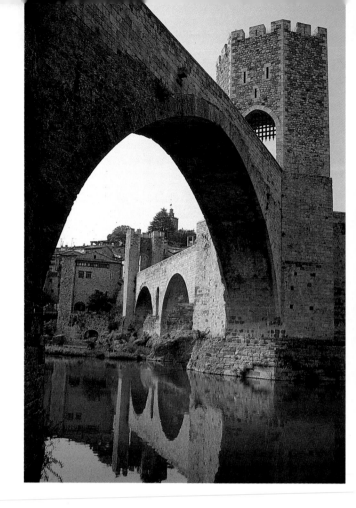

Above, left to right: A twelfth-century Romanesque church at Porqueres. An impressive fortified bridge marks the entrance to the town of Besalú. *Below:* Many believers come to Montserrat Monastery to pay homage to *La Moreneta,* the venerated Black Virgin who is Catalonia's patron saint.

Right: This waterfront monument commemorates the moment when a triumphant Columbus sailed into Barcelona after his first successful expedition to the New World. *Below:* Just opposite Barcelona's Columbus Monument is a replica of the *Santa María*.

Constructed for the 1929 World's Fair, the *Palau Nacional* in Barcelona houses the *Museu d'Art de Catalunya*. *Below:* One of Barcelona's urban focal points is the *Plaza de España*.

Between Barcelona's *Plaza de España* and *Palau Nacional* stand the twin Venetian Towers marking the *Feria de Barcelona*, the city's convention complex. *Below:* The core collection of Barcelona's *Fundació Joan Miró* follows this Catalan abstractionist's work from 1914 to 1978.

When it comes to wines, the appellations are many and growing. Oenophiles rejoice in the robust reds and fresh whites of Rioja, the subtle reds and fragrant whites of the Penedés, the sparkling whites of Galicia, the fine *cavas* ("champagnes") of Catalonia, the hearty "black" wines of the Pyrenees, and the sophisticated sherries and brandies of Andalusia.

A toast, then, to Spain, which has given the world a good many things. Cervantes and the novel. The far-reaching artistic vision of Velázquez, Goya, Picasso and Miró. The architectural daring of Gaudí. Columbus Day and the Americas (North and South). The legends of *conquistadores,* the lure of sunken treasure, and a language that is today among the most widely spoken in the world. Not bad for a country significantly smaller than the state of Texas.

This page, top to bottom: Architecture is a Barcelona passion and modernist architect Antoni Gaudí left his mark here at *Parc Güell* as well as elsewhere throughout the city. Between the port and the *Plaza de Cataluña* stretches Barcelona's famed *Ramblas,* where the passing parade of humanity runs from the seedy to the sublime. Barcelona is bullish on business and commerce; note its imposing Trade Center. *Opposite:* Of bombastic, medieval proportions is Gaudí's unfinished *Sagrada Familia* cathedral, Barcelona's most well-known landmark.

This page: Whimsical, intricate, and intensely symbolic, the spires and elaborate ornamentation of the *Sagrada Familia* might best be described as "gingerbread Gothic."

nother Gaudí grace note is Barcelona's *Casa Battló,* which now houses an insurance company. *Below:* Gaudí's undulating *Casa Milá* opularly referred to as *La Pedrera*), built between 1905 and 1910, was his last completed work.

These pages: Within the refurbished 1929 facade of Barcelona's Olympic Stadium is a brand new arena that seats 70,000. Barcelona's core Olympic Complex occupies the seaside hill of Montjuïc.

Index of Photography

All photos courtesy of The Image Bank,
except where indicated *.